COUNTING

AT THE ZOO

Please visit our web site at: **www.garethstevens.com**
For a free color catalog describing our list of high-quality books,
call 1-800-542-2595 (USA) or 1-800-387-3178 (Canada).

Library of Congress Cataloging-in-Publication Data

Rauen, Amy.
    Counting at the zoo / Amy Rauen. — North American ed.
      p. cm. — (Math in our world)
    ISBN-13: 978-0-8368-8469-2 (lib. bdg.)
    ISBN-10: 0-8368-8469-8 (lib. bdg.)
    ISBN-13: 978-0-8368-8478-4 (softcover)
    ISBN-10: 0-8368-8478-7 (softcover)
    1. Counting—Juvenile literature. 2. Animals—Juvenile literature.
3. Zoo—Juvenile literature. I. Title.
QA113.R378 2008
513.2'11—dc22   2007017943

This edition first published in 2008 by
Weekly Reader® Books
An imprint of Gareth Stevens Publishing
1 Reader's Digest Road
Pleasantville, NY 10570-7000 USA

Copyright © 2008 by Gareth Stevens, Inc.

Managing editor: Dorothy L. Gibbs
Art direction: Tammy West

Photo credits: cover, pp. 3, 22 © Gary D. Landsman/Corbis; p. 4 © Nik Wheeler/Corbis;
p. 5 © William Manning/Corbis; p. 6 © Lon C. Diehl/Photo Edit; p. 7 Adam Jones/
Visuals Unlimited/Getty Images; p. 8 U.S. Fish and Wildlife Service; p. 9 Raymond Gehman/
National Geographic/Getty Images; p. 10 © Wolfgang Kaehler/Corbis; pp. 11, 24 (top left)
© Mark Newman/FLPA; p. 12 © Jim Merli/Visuals Unlimited; pp. 13, 24 (bottom left)
© David Hosking/FLPA; p. 14 Russell Pickering; p. 15 © Inga Spence/Visuals Unlimited;
pp. 16, 24 (bottom right) © Klaus Hackenberg/zefa/Corbis; p. 17 © Warren Morgan/Corbis;
p. 18 © Mary Kate Denny/Photo Edit; p. 19 © Galen Rowell/Corbis; p. 20 Nina Buesing/Stone+/
Getty Images; p. 21 © Eric Wanders/Foto Natura/FLPA; pp. 23, 24 (top right) Guy Edwardes/
The Image Bank/Getty Images.

Printed in the United States of America

1 2 3 4 5 6 7 8 9 11 10 09 08 07

MATH IN OUR WORLD

COUNTING

AT THE ZOO

by Amy Rauen

Reading consultant: Susan Nations, M.Ed.,
author/literacy coach/consultant in literacy development
Math consultant: Rhea Stewart, M.A., mathematics content specialist

WEEKLY READER®
PUBLISHING

Aunt Nina took me to the zoo.

I like the zoo.
It is a fun place.

The zoo has many animals.

We counted animals all day.
1, 2, 3 lions!

We saw 2 owls.

We saw 7 deer.

We saw more deer than owls.

We saw 6 seals.

We saw 3 bears.
We saw fewer bears than seals.

We saw 8 turtles.

We saw 11 bats.
We saw more bats than turtles.

Aunt Nina and I got hungry.
We ate lunch.

We ate near a pond.

Then we saw 14 ducks.

Next we saw 9 fish.
We saw fewer fish than ducks.

We saw 4 chimps.

We saw 10 penguins.
We saw more penguins than chimps.

We saw 20 sheep.

We saw 18 storks.
We saw fewer storks than sheep.

Then we looked for snakes.
We saw 0 snakes.

We saw 4 wolves last.
We saw more wolves than snakes.

Glossary

fewer – There are fewer bears than wolves.

more – There are more ducks than bats.

About the Author

Amy Rauen is the author of thirteen math books for children. She also designs and writes educational software. Amy lives in San Diego, California, with her husband and their two cats.